FAMILIES LEARNING TOGETHER

BOOK 1: JESUS' EARLY LIFE

Cover design by Brian Lovell
Inside illustrations by Rusty Fletcher
Design and typography by Liz Howe
Project editor, Ruth Frederick

All Scripture quotations, unless otherwise indicated, are taken from the HOLY BIBLE,
NEW INTERNATIONAL VERSION®. NIV®. Copyright © 1973, 1978, 1984 by International Bible Society.
Used by permission of Zondervan Publishing House. All rights reserved.

The Standard Publishing Company, Cincinnati, Ohio
A division of Standex International Corporation

©1998 Karyn Henley
All rights reserved.
Exclusively administered by the Institute of Child Sensitive Communication, LLC.
Printed in the United States of America

05 04 03 02 01 00 99 98   5 4 3 2 1

ISBN 0-784-70921-1

Material may not be reproduced in whole or in part in any form or format
(except where permission is given) without special permission from the publisher.

Contents

Introduction 5

■ ■ ■

Looking for Jesus to Come 17

God's Gift 20

Gifts for Baby Jesus 23

Recognizing Jesus 26

Obedience 29

Who Is Jesus? 32

Temptation and the Choices We Make 35

Jesus Calls His Disciples 38

Revival, the Waking Up 41

Knowing Jesus 44

Worship and Praise 47

Failure 50

Prayer, the Power Line 53

Persecution 56

Letting Your Light Shine 59

Introduction

Home groups. Cell groups. Care groups. Family groups. Community groups. These are some of the names for small gatherings of church members meeting together weekly in homes. Many church leaders have found these meetings to be an effective way to provide caring relationships for church members as well as being an effective format for evangelism. Membership in these groups can be quite diverse. One group may include couples, singles, older adults, and families with a variety of ages of children. And often, the question that is foremost in their minds is, "What do we do with the children?"

■ ■ ■

HOW DO I USE THIS GUIDE?

THE DECISION IS YOURS!
If you want step-by-step structure, you can follow each lesson as written. But remember:
> The structure was created to serve you.
> You were not created to serve the structure.
> That's where your decisions come in.

WHAT DECISIONS?
Decide which Building Blocks to use.

WHY?
Some of them may not fit your group's needs.
You may want to do things in a different order.
You may want to leave out a block or two.
You may want to add a block of your own.

So, choose the blocks you need, in the order you need.
    * This block requires kids and adults together.
  ** This block requires kids to separate from the adults. However, do provide two adults to facilitate.
    + Options:
      1. Do with kids and adults OR
      2. Do with kids only.

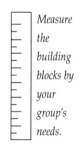

Measure the building blocks by your group's needs.

Add or delete as needed.

WHAT SHOULD I KNOW ABOUT THIS GUIDEBOOK?

GOAL: to help children and adults develop and exercise faith in God the Father, the Son, and the Holy Spirit.

ADAPTABILITY: This guide is yours, so be flexible.
- Feel free *not* to follow the order of the lessons. Skip around, if you like.
- You may want to stay close to a subject your pastor has emphasized in a large assembly. For example, if your pastor has given a lesson on prayer, you may want to use one of the lessons on prayer, even though you are going out of sequence.

CHOICES: Don't try to do every activity. You'll only have time for one, maybe two. See page 8 for other decisions you may want to consider.

AGE SPAN: It is for multiage groups of kids in an intergenerational setting. There are activities for all ages of children. Older children are encouraged to help the younger children when necessary, in family-style cooperation.

MATERIALS: All items listed are commonly found in most households or are readily available at the nearest grocery or discount store.

IMPORTANT: Again, this is a collection of suggestions. As with any teaching guide, you may change it to suit your particular needs. This guide is quite structured to help those who rely on specific steps spelled out. Feel free to change it in any way you need to.

WHAT DO I DO WITH THE CHILDREN?

One of the first questions to be asked about cells and home groups is, "What do you do with the children?" That is a very good question. Place the emphasis on the word *with*. "What do you do *with* the children?"

If you want to reap the richest rewards from your group, include the children. Be a family. Once you worship *with* children, do an object lesson or activity *with* children, snack and fellowship *with* children, you'll find out that God has planned all along for them to do for you much more than you had ever imagined!

So, *what* do we do with our children? We show them they belong. We value them. We treat them as part of the group, which is an extended family.

WHY INCLUDE THE CHILDREN?
1. To promote family togetherness. The family in our society is broken. Time for developing family relationships is preempted by school, sports, lessons, work, TV. Malachi wrote, "See, I will send you the prophet Elijah before that great and dreadful day of the Lord comes. He will turn the hearts of the fathers to their children, and the hearts of the children to their fathers; or else I will come and strike the land with a curse" (Malachi 4:5, 6). This guide is to help facilitate parent-child interaction.

2. Parents will know what their children are learning and will be able to build on the teaching during the week. This places the responsibility where it should be: parents teaching their children about life in the Lord.

3. Adults will be reached by participating in the children's lessons. We touch their hearts by going in the back door so to speak. Adults often think they are observing or helping out when they watch and listen to someone teaching children. Then they realize that the spiritual truth, presented so simply, has impacted their lives in a memorable way.

4. Children can minister to adults too. They can pray powerful prayers for adults. They can come up with profound insights. God uses them. They are not the future church. They are part of the church today.

5. Single adults often long for "connectedness." They often struggle with loneliness, and for that reason, they enjoy being with families. "God sets the lonely in families" (Psalm 68:6). It is also good for singles and young couples to watch the loving interaction between parents and children. Single adults can sometimes give children special attention that children long for.

HOW DO WE SHOW THEM THEY BELONG?
We develop a meaningful relationship with them. It's the best way to make a difference in their lives.

HOW DO WE DEVELOP A MEANINGFUL RELATIONSHIP WITH THEM?
We listen to them. We *do* things with them. We play with them. Hemfelt and Warren, in their book *Kids Who Carry our Pain*, tell us "play is the single most effective way to communicate with children less than nine years old."

WHEN DO THE ADULTS GET TO TALK AND SHARE TOGETHER WITHOUT THE CHILDREN?
Adults do need time to share concerns with other adults. Children need time away from adults in the group too. So after spending some time gathered as a large group, you will want to separate and allow time for kids and adults to continue separately. Decide when this time will be according to your group's needs. See options on page 5.

WHO TAKES CHARGE OF THE CHILDREN'S TIME?
Take turns. Rotate each week, so each adult can get to know the children, and the children can get to know each adult. Anyone who feels uncomfortable working with the children can be an assistant for awhile to another adult who is perhaps more familiar with children.

It is best to have at least two people working with the children. Older children can help the younger, just as in a real family. This helps both the older and younger child feel valued.

WHAT SHOULD I KNOW ABOUT CHILDREN?
1. The younger the child, the shorter his attention span will be. Most kids have a hard time sitting still for more than ten minutes at a time, less than that for young ones.

2. The more of their five senses you involve, the greater the possibility that they will remember. Some learn best by simply hearing, but most learn best by seeing and doing.

3. Children younger than 8 or 9 do not understand symbolism and do not have a good perspective of time and history.

4. Decide on rules of conduct. Let the children know what those rules are. Link responsibility (to behave properly) with privileges (joining the activity, snack, and so on). Be consistent in enforcing the rules and encourage those who misbehave that you are confident they'll do better next time.

WHAT ABOUT TEENS?

Your group will have to decide. Some groups like to continue to preserve the family togetherness by involving the teens with the family's cell group. Teens can be in charge of the story time. If there are few teens, they can help with the younger children when the kids and adults separate. If there are several teens, they can form a third group to share their concerns and pray for each other.

Other groups encourage teens to have special teen cells entirely separate from the family cells.

HOW DO WE DO THIS? GIVE ME SPECIFICS.

Feel free to
- take lessons out of order.
- do the segments of the lesson in any order.
- leave out any portion of the lesson.
- choose only one or two of the activities.

NOW, LET'S INSPECT EACH BUILDING BLOCK.

I. WORSHIP (songs and praise)
Encourage children to suggest songs and to lead songs sometimes. Children will also enjoy singing energetic songs and songs with hand motions.

II. STORY (optional)
If you have all heard your pastor speak on a certain passage, you may want simply to refer to what everyone has heard and then move on to a memory verse or activity that would be appropriate.

If you need a story, you will find suggestions in each lesson for ways to tell the story. Some are object lessons. You can choose one adult to be in charge of the story time each week, or let adults take turns. You do not have to use the suggestions given. Feel free to tell the story your own way. Children can even tell the story or read the passage. But try not to do the same thing every week. Vary the approach to keep it interesting and fun.

III. MEMORY VERSE (optional)
Most verses are short. Explain any words children may not understand. Each memory verse includes a song or active method to help children remember the Scripture. Give parents an index card and ask them to write the verse on the card so they can take it home with them and continue to review the verse during the week as a family.

There may be children who come without their parents. In that case, another child can get together with this child during the following week, either by phone or in person, and help him review his memory verse.

IV. ACTIVITIES
A variety of activities are suggested. You will only be able to do one or two of them. Vary the type of activity from week to week. Choose activities according to the abilities, interests, and needs of the specific children in your group. Let older children and adults help the younger ones.

You will find suggestions for discussion included with most activities. There is also a list of questions after the activity section. During the activity, while hands are busy, use these questions to guide discussion toward the concepts you want everyone to discover and think about.

V. KIDS' COUNCIL
Try to make this time special by your attitude and the atmosphere you set, so the children feel like the focus is on them and their needs. You can sit together on the floor or ground if that helps make it a special time. Or you may choose a special room or corner that the children can feel is their own. You may even want to have Kids' Council in a clubhouse or tent.

1. **Bring It Home.** Apply the Scripture and activity to their daily lives in the coming week. Questions are suggested for you.
2. **Share and Pray.** Sometimes the previous discussion with the children will expose prayer needs. At other times, children may have very different needs. Share answers to prayers that you've prayed in past weeks. Let children pray for each other.
3. **Extra.** As needed, do another activity (section IV), or allow free play. Play with the children to strengthen your relationship.

VI. ADULT STUDY QUESTIONS
While the children are having a special time together, adults will want to share their needs with each other. The study questions allow adults to go deeper into the theme of the lesson. The questions are meant to be a challenge and lead into thoughtful discussion. But if your group has other needs, you will want to skip the study questions so you can share those needs and pray for each other.

VII. SNACK AND FELLOWSHIP TIME
You may wish to have this time at another point in the meeting. The advantage of having it at the end is that it gives you the option of letting the children prepare and serve the snack.

HOUSE RULES
A home group is like an extended family. Just as a family has practical guidelines for behavior, your group can also have guidelines. It is helpful if everyone in the *group* is aware of the guidelines. If these are group guidelines, then there is an understanding that everyone will remind one another that "this is the way we behave in our group."

Generally, there should be only a few rules, and they should be stated in the positive. See the examples shown.

Remember that children younger than 4 need to be reminded often, and wiggliness and a short attention span are not misbehaviors.

House Rules

1. We speak kind words.
2. We keep our feet off the furniture.
3. We walk indoors (not run).
4. We use quiet, indoor voices inside the house.
5. We help clean up. We put away any toys we get out.

You may find it helpful to write your rules on a poster. Or you may want to use a group meeting time to list the ways everyone agrees to behave. Let all the children sign this list as a contract or agreement to abide by the guidelines.

Rules usually fall into three basic categories:
1. Honoring God
2. Respecting and encouraging others
3. Respecting property

These may be the only guidelines you want to write down. It will be helpful for children if you discuss each one briefly and let them tell you how they can achieve each rule and what behaviors might be considered violations of the rules.

Children can also give suggestions for what the consequences for violating the rules might be. Generally, effective consequences are
- removing the privilege that the behavior is abusing.
- removing the child from the group for a period of time.
- removing material that is being abused or that is being used to hurt others or property.

Sometimes children misbehave when they are in situations in which it is unclear who the authority is. It may be helpful to let everyone know that
1. when you meet as a large group (adults and children together), the parents are in charge of their own child's behavior.

2. when children and adults meet separately, the people who are supervising the children are the ones to be obeyed. They will enforce the rules.

3. the person at whose house you are meeting has the last word on what is or is not out of bounds for their house. It will help if doors are closed to any room that is off limits and if fragile or treasured objects are put in safe places.

For suggestions on dealing with misbehavior, see the eight-page folder *Behavior Management* or the book *Child-Sensitive Teaching* (Standard Publishing).

If you have problems with certain specific behaviors, it is very appropriate to discuss it in a group meeting and help each other decide on the best way to handle it. Remember that you may not immediately arrive at a solution that will work. If what you try doesn't seem to be working, try something else.

INVOLVING CHILDREN WITH ADULTS

THE SITUATION

In the beginning, God created family. Older family members taught the younger family members through example and counsel. Younger family members challenged the thinking of older family members and were often a source of joy as the older members watched them grow stronger and wiser. Older people were comfortable being around the younger ones. Little ones were comfortable interacting with the older generations.

But in our society today, children spend most of their time with peer groups. Adults spend much of their time with adults. So it is not unusual for adults to feel bothered and impatient with children whose needs they do not understand. And it is not unusual for children, especially older children, to feel impatient and bothered with adults.

THE NEEDS

In order to form an intergenerational group, you will need adults who are willing to move out of the traditional peer-oriented comfort zone. They will need to be

- **Patient**
  If this is the first time adults and children have been in an intergenerational group, do not expect everything to flow smoothly at first. The children will have to get used to what is happening and what is expected of them. The adults will have to get used to a group whose members may wiggle more and make more noise.

- **Willing to Learn**
  In the intergenerational group, everyone comes to learn together. Adults don't come in order to pour their knowledge into children. Instead, they establish an atmosphere where everyone learns together. Adults ask and listen and guide. An intergenerational group challenges everyone's thinking.

- **Good Examples**
  Children don't know what it's like to be an adult, so they watch and listen to adults. Adults in the intergenerational group need to be aware that younger eyes are watching them, and younger ears are listening to them. The adults in the group are teaching more by their example. They are modeling life as a follower of Jesus.

- **Willing to Love and Encourage**
  One of the primary benefits of family is the love and encouragement that can be given to each other. Being family is . . .

  > . . . being valued and respected for who you are.
  > . . . being able to contribute to the welfare of the family unit.
  > . . . being accountable to people who care about you.
  > . . . being able to make mistakes and still be loved anyway.
  > . . . being able to talk and be listened to.
  > . . . being encouraged and not discouraged.
  > . . . being prayed for day in and day out.

- **Willing to Sacrifice Self-Interest for the Interests of Others**
  In God's kingdom, those who give up their lives find true life. Those who cling to their lives lose life. It takes work to mature in a family. It takes thinking and praying and giving up self. It means doing the difficult. It means giving up current pleasure in order to receive future rewards.

So "let us throw off everything that hinders and the sin that so easily entangles, and let us run with perseverance the race marked out for us. Let us fix our eyes on Jesus, the author and perfecter of our faith, who for the joy set before him endured the cross, scorning its shame, and sat down at the right hand of the throne of God" (Hebrews 12:1, 2).

HOW GOD MADE US

INFANTS
- are self-centered
- depend on others to care for them
- learn through their senses
- focus on the present
- do not make conscious choices between right and wrong
- are sensitive to tone of voice

If you have infants in your group,
- they will enjoy listening to your group sing.
- they will enjoy holding and chewing on their toys.
- they may want to be with mom and/or dad.
- or they may be happy being held by someone else.
- they can stay with the adults during Kids' Council, or they can go with the children if an older child will help care for them.
- they may want someone to hold them and walk them around the room during parts of your group time.
- let them feel the atmosphere of love, joy, and peace, so they will know this is a safe, loving place.
- you can introduce infants to God by saying: "God made (whatever they are eating, touching)." "God takes care of you" (when you are taking care of them). "God loves you" (when you are rocking or snuggling with them).

EARLY CHILDHOOD: Ages 2 and 3
- are wanting to be more independent
- may have strong wills
- have short attention spans
- sit still for only a few minutes
- want to know that mom and/or dad are nearby
- are still self-centered and self-focused
- learn by touching and doing
- play *beside* but not cooperatively with other children
- need to know what the rules are
- need patient, consistent training from adults
- need to be able to do some things for themselves
- get fantasy and reality mixed up
- do not understand the flow of time
- do not understand symbolism or figures of speech
- imitate the faith of significant adults around them

12

If you have toddlers in your group,
- be prepared to let them wiggle.
- try to find ways that they can help.
- let them play a rhythm instrument when you sing.
- let them move into and out of the activities as their attention ebbs and flows.
- give them things to touch and do.
- ask older children to help them as big sisters and brothers help their younger siblings.
- be patient.
- let them hold a small sturdy book for a songbook and a Bible so they can imitate you.
- let them go with the other children to Kids' Council, but be ready to let them go back in with the adults to get the assurance that mom and dad are still nearby.
- have extra toddler toys for them to play with.

EARLY CHILDHOOD: Ages 4 and 5
- enjoy exploring and discovering
- are usually very active
- ask many, many questions
- learn by touching and doing
- still have a short attention span, although it's getting longer
- need to know what the rules are
- are beginning to be more self-controlled because their conscience is now developing
- can begin to be aware that they sin
- get fantasy and reality mixed up
- do not understand the flow of time
- do not understand symbolism and figures of speech
- imitate the faith of the significant adults around them
- realize that they are growing and getting older
- now play *with* and not just beside other children
- want to help and like to surprise people with their good deeds

If you have four and five year olds in your group,
- actively involve them as much as possible.
- explain symbolic concepts and language in simple ways, relating it to something they know.
- let them choose and lead some songs.
- choose touching and doing activities, as well as activities that fit their abilities.
- enjoy their curiosity.
- tell them how proud you are that they are getting so big and growing up.
- acknowledge and compliment their efforts.
- listen to them.
- let them use songbooks and Bibles for preschoolers.
- be patient.
- point out that the Bible stories really happened.
- help them without making them feel incapable.
- provide ways for them to help.

ELEMENTARY: Ages 6 through 10

- want to be busy doing productive things
- enjoy projects
- like to show their skills and abilities
- want to feel like a valued member of a group
- want to hear adults' testimonies about how God is working in their lives
- want to tell about what God is doing in their own lives
- sit still longer but may still wiggle
- learn best by touching and doing and seeing visual aids
- easily feel inferior if they are put down or if they feel incapable
- are seeing their need for a Savior
- can be very sensitive to spiritual issues
- want to see how God is real and how he relates to everyday life
- have a growing understanding of symbolism
- understand the flow of time
- are concerned about what's fair and just
- are more consistent about discerning right from wrong
- memorize more easily

If you have elementary age children in your group,

- treat them as full-fledged members.
- ask them about their schools, sports and other interests, and listen with interest.
- let them take an active part in group discussions, activities, preparations, and cleanup.
- involve them in service projects with your group.
- try to utilize their skills and abilities.
- let the older children help with the younger.
- encourage them to pursue their own relationship with the Lord through Bible reading and prayer.
- ask adults to tell how God is working in their lives.
- let children tell about God working in their lives.
- help them apply the spiritual lessons you discuss in your group to their daily lives.
- compliment their efforts.

LEADING A CHILD TO JESUS

Each child is a unique individual. So the best way to know a particular child's spiritual level is to listen to him and observe him. This requires developing a relationship with him. Developing relationships is one of the blessings of intergenerational groups. The preceding pages have given a foundation of important facts that help us lead children to Jesus. Here is a review.

- **Self and Sin.** Children are born self-focused. Since self is the basis of sin, we can say that children are born sinful. But in their first few years, they're not aware that they sin.
- **Right and Wrong.** As children get close to two years old, they begin exhibiting a strong will. They want some independence in decision making but are not mature enough to make consistent decisions between right and wrong. In fact, they decide what's right and wrong by knowing whether they'll be rewarded or punished for certain behaviors.
- **Awareness of Others.** Around three years old, children reach a major milestone: becoming aware that other people have possessions, opinions, and needs. They begin to see how their choices affect others.
- **The Conscience.** The four-year-old child reaches another major milestone. His conscience begins to develop. This guides more of his choices. Now he can understand that he sometimes makes the wrong choice. This awareness allows him to say, "I am a sinner," and he can begin to see the need for a Savior.
- **Fantasy and Reality.** Everything a young child experiences gets stirred into one big world in his brain, interpreted largely by imagination. Spiritual concepts and Bible stories get mixed in with cartoon stories and super heroes. But around age five, children begin distinguishing fantasy from reality. They can know that the salvation message is real.
- **Death and Life.** Young children have a hard time telling what is alive and what is not. Until they are about five or six, they will not understand what it means when we say that Jesus died.
- **Symbolism.** When children are six or seven, they begin to understand symbolism. In fact, some people call the child's seventh year "the age of reason." This is significant, because many of the methods we use to tell the salvation message are symbolic.
- **Seeing a Need.** Elementary age children begin feeling a need for God's help as they face their everyday lives.

SO AT WHAT AGE CAN A CHILD RECEIVE JESUS AS HIS LORD AND SAVIOR?

He can learn to love Jesus and believe in him very early. Then he must see that he sins and needs a Savior. He must be willing to let Jesus be his Lord, his Boss, his King. How much do children have to understand? That's a good question. But God never asks us to understand. He just asks us to obey. And that's something even a child can do.

THE SALVATION MESSAGE IS REALLY VERY SIMPLE.

- God is perfect. He never does wrong.
- God does not allow anything bad, wrong, or imperfect to be around him.
- We are not perfect. Even if we try to be perfect, we sometimes make the wrong choice. We lie, or say bad words, or throw a fit, or take things that really aren't ours.
- Since we are not perfect, we cannot be around God. We will never be able to live with him where there's no hurting or crying or dying, where there's joy and peace and love forever.
- But God loves us and wants us to be able to live with him. So he sent Jesus, his Son. Jesus was a man, a human like we are, except for one thing: he was perfect.
- So Jesus traded with us. He took our sins, our wrongs. And he was punished for all the bad things we've done or will do. He was killed on a cross.

- So Jesus took our sins and gave us his perfectness. If we say YES to Jesus, if we tell him we will let him be our Savior (to save us from the punishment our sin would bring us), then we get his perfectness. We become perfect in God's kingdom, and we will get to live with joy and peace and love forevermore.
- In fact, there's more good news: God brought Jesus back to life again, and now Jesus is preparing a place for us with him in heaven.
- And there's even more good news: When we let Jesus be our Savior and our Lord (our Boss, our King), he sends his Holy Spirit to live inside us. In that way, Jesus can always be with us. The Holy Spirit puts joy and peace in our hearts. He teaches us and leads us and tells us God's thoughts. He helps us become all that Jesus wants us to be.

SESSION 1

Looking for Jesus to Come

OBJECTIVE: *To realize that God always fulfills his promises, sometimes in ways we might consider impossible.*

■ ■ ■

WORSHIP

Sing songs that are meaningful and familiar to your group, especially those that relate to the promise that God made to his prophets long ago. Here are some suggestions.

"Arise and Sing"
"Come, Thou Long-Expected Jesus"
"For Unto Us a Child Is Born" (Isaiah 9:6; 7:14)
"Great Is Thy Faithfulness"
"I Will Sing of the Mercies of the Lord"
"O Come, O Come, Emmanuel" (Isaiah 7:14)
"Wonderful, Wonderful Jesus Is to Me" (Isaiah 9:6)

STORY

The Angel Tells Mary About the Coming Birth of Jesus, Luke 1:26-38
■ The angel Gabriel appears to Mary.
■ Gabriel tells Mary that she will be the mother of God's Son.
■ Mary says she will do God's will.

Draw in the dark. Give each person paper and a pencil or crayon. Turn off the lights. While you tell the story, everyone else tries to draw an angel in the dark. Then turn on the lights and let everyone show each other what they've drawn. Talk about Jesus being the "true light" for the world (John 1:9). Ask: "What does that mean?"

MEMORY VERSE

"Nothing is impossible with God" (Luke 1:37).

To help everyone remember the verse, sing it to the tune of "The Ants Go Marching One by One" (page 19). Repeat as many times as you wish. To end the song, add "amen" at the end.

17

ACTIVITIES

Choose one or more of the following activities to support the story or theme and to provide a springboard for discussion.

ANGEL PUPPETS. Give each person a plastic spoon. On the bowl of the spoon, each person draws a face with a permanent marker. Supervise young children. Fold a piece of plain white paper accordion-style. Tape the center of the folded paper to the handle of the spoon beneath the face to make wings. Hold the handle of the spoon to fly the angel puppet.

BOW JEWELRY. Give each person a stick-on gift wrap bow and a length of string or yarn, about 34 inches for a necklace, 12 inches for a bracelet. Take the protective paper off the bow sticker. Lay the center of the string across it. Cut a piece of plain paper to be the size of the protective paper. Place this piece of paper on top of the string, sandwiching the string between the paper and the bow. Tie the ends of the string to fit loosely around the person's neck or wrist. Talk about the gift that the angel told Mary about.

JESUS IS. On paper, each person can glue letter-shaped dry cereal to spell JESUS IS. Then he chooses a name for the promised Son of God and glues on cereal to spell that name, or writes the name with a marker. Some suggestions can be Immanuel (Isaiah 7:14), Wonderful Counselor, Mighty God, Everlasting Father, Prince of Peace (Isaiah 9:6). Or they may choose other words, such as Lord, Master, Savior, Son of God. Talk about God's plan announced to Mary.

SENDING A MESSAGE. Choose a Sender. Give him an envelope. The Sender says, "I'm sending a message by *(he names another person)* Express. I'm sending it over the sand." The person he named must come to the Sender and get the envelope, pretending to walk on sand. Then he walks back to his own seat the same way, and he becomes the Sender. The Sender always calls a person's name and how that person will have to travel (over snow, ice, mud, rain puddles, a hot sidewalk, and so on). Talk about the different ways we send messages today and how God sent his message to Mary.

QUESTIONS

1. When do you say, "I can hardly wait"? What kinds of things are you waiting for when you say that?
2. Can you think of some Scriptures from long before Jesus was born that told about Jesus' coming? (Isaiah 7:14; 9:1-7; 11:1-3; Micah 5:2)
3. Who were some of the people waiting for Jesus to come?
4. What are some things you can do while you are waiting for something?
5. What do you like best about the story of Jesus' birth?

KIDS' COUNCIL

BRING IT HOME
- Some people who celebrate Christmas do not believe in Jesus. Do you know someone like this?
- How can you share your faith with them this year?
- How can you help them know about Jesus?

SHARE AND PRAY
- Ask the children to pray for each other.
- Pray for the people the children mentioned above.
- Ask God for the courage to share their faith with these people. Ask God to draw these people to Jesus.

ADULT STUDY QUESTIONS
- What are some of the obstacles that Mary might have faced if this story had taken place in today's world? What obstacles did she face in her day?
- What arguments could Mary have made mentally as to why this message could not be true?
- Have you ever felt that God was wanting you to do something that you thought was impossible? What were the obstacles?
- Do you really believe that "nothing is impossible with God," or are there some qualifications to this statement?
- Tell about something that God has done that would seem impossible in the eyes of the world.

SNACK AND FELLOWSHIP

Hot Cider. Let children mix together:

1 quart apple juice	1 quart cranberry juice
2 tablespoons lemon juice	1 stick cinnamon
3 cloves	¼ teaspoon allspice
¼ teaspoon nutmeg	

Heat to boiling, strain and serve. Discuss waiting. Say: "We have to wait for foods to cook. We have to wait for Christmas. Who was waiting for Jesus to be born?" (More people than just Mary and Joseph.)

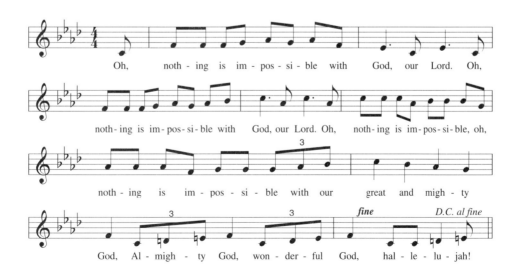

SESSION 2

God's Gift

OBJECTIVE: *To contemplate the significance of why Jesus came.*

■ ■ ■

WORSHIP

Sing songs about Jesus' birth that are meaningful and familiar to your group. Here are some suggestions.

"Angels We Have Heard on High"
"Away in a Manger"
"Hark! the Herald Angels Sing"
"O Little Town of Bethlehem"
"Silent Night"
"The First Noel"

STORY

The Birth of Jesus, Luke 2:1-20

■ Jesus is born in a stable in Bethlehem.
■ Angels announce Jesus' birth to shepherds.
■ Shepherds visit the baby in Bethlehem.

Bring a baby doll. Assign parts for the characters in the story. Children act out the nativity story as you read or narrate it. Or ask a child to read or narrate. Then everyone can sing carols together.

Option: While adults meet, the children can plan and practice the presentation of the story. Then before snack time, children join the adult group again to present their nativity play.

MEMORY VERSE

"For God so loved the world that he gave his one and only Son, that whoever believes in him shall not perish but have eternal life" (John 3:16).

To help the children remember the verse, use hand motions.

For God so loved the world (hands over heart)
that he gave his one and only Son (one finger up)
that who**ev**er be**lieves** in **him** (tap temple with forefinger on the syllables in bold)
shall not perish but have eternal life (spread arms out wide, side to side)

Discuss the meaning of the words *perish* and *eternal.*

ACTIVITIES

Choose one or more of the following activities to support the story or theme and to provide a springboard for discussion.

CANDY CANE NAME. Give each person a paper plate and a candy cane. Show everyone how to turn the candy cane upside down to make a J. Spell the name JESUS by gluing the J to the left of the center of the plate and write ESUS to the right of the J. Read what the angel told Joseph in Matthew 1:21. Talk about why Jesus came.

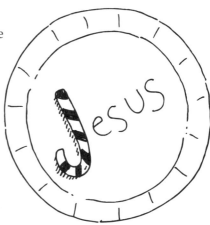

BIRTH ANNOUNCEMENT. Talk about what a birth announcement is. Let each person make one on a piece of gift-wrapping paper. They write on the white side, "Jesus Is Born!" Then fold the paper like a greeting card with the message inside. Talk about how Jesus' birth was announced to Mary, Elizabeth, and Joseph.

CLOTH ANGELS. Give each person a square of soft cloth the size of a handkerchief or bandanna. Lay it flat in front of them. Show them how to roll the right and left sides toward each other to meet in the middle like a scroll. Fold the top of this scroll down halfway. You are working on the back of the angel. Tie it a few inches from the fold with gift wrap ribbon to make a head. The short rolls are arms, the long rolls are legs. Pull the fabric between the short rolls up and over the "head" to make wings. Turn the angel over to see the front. Draw eyes and mouth if you want. Talk about messages the angel brought in Luke 1, 2.

NATIVITY. Children act out the nativity story for parents. Everyone sings carols together.

BOW PICTURE. Give each person a piece of paper and a self-stick gift wrap bow. Let everyone stick the bow on the paper. Write on it, "I am a gift from God to my family." Talk about John 3:16 and the gift God gave.

QUESTIONS

1. What makes Christmas special for you and your family?
2. Why do we celebrate Christmas? Why do we give gifts?
3. Why did Jesus come? (Read John 3:16.)
4. What do you think Jesus had to give up to come to the earth? (Read Philippians 2:6, 7.)
5. Is there anything you have to give up for him?

KIDS' COUNCIL

BRING IT HOME
- What can you give besides something you buy?
- Think of something you can do for someone this week. Doing things for people is a way of giving.

SHARE AND PRAY
- Encourage children to pray for each other.
- Pray a prayer thanking God for the gift of his only Son.
- Children may want to pray to ask Jesus to be their Lord and Savior.

ADULT STUDY QUESTIONS
- Why do you think John 3:16 has become such a well-known verse?
- Read John 3:17, 18. If God didn't send Jesus into the world to condemn the world, why do so many people feel that God is a condemning God? Compare what these verses really say to the way the world has twisted the concepts of salvation and condemnation.
- Discuss Philippians 2:5–11. Verse 5 says we should have the attitude of Jesus that verses 6–8 describe. How can that attitude be lived out in our lives today?

SNACK AND FELLOWSHIP

Candy Cane Cupcakes. Mix and bake cupcakes from a boxed cake mix, any flavor. Frost the cupcakes and place a small candy cane on top so that it forms the letter J. Discuss the meaning of the J as suggested in the activity "Candy Cane Name."

SESSION 3

Gifts for Baby Jesus

OBJECTIVE: *To consider why Jesus is such a wonderful gift from God and to decide what we can give God in return.*

■ ■ ■

WORSHIP

Sing songs about Jesus' birth that are familiar and meaningful to your group. Here are some suggestions.
"Do You See What I See?"
"Go Tell It on the Mountain"
"O Come, All Ye Faithful"
"We Bow Down"
"We Three Kings"
"What Child Is This?"

STORY

The Wise Men Bring Gifts to Baby Jesus, Matthew 2
■ Wise men following a special star go to Jerusalem and ask for the baby king.
■ Wise men travel to Bethlehem to see baby Jesus.
■ God tells the wise men to travel home a different way.

Copy the text of the story. Cut it into three sections. Wrap each section in a separate box, complete with bow. Number the boxes 1, 2, and 3, with the first, second, and third sections of the story in the corresponding boxes. Choose three people to receive each box. The person with box #1 opens it and reads that Scripture. Then #2 opens and reads his Scripture. Then #3 opens and reads his Scripture.

MEMORY VERSE

"For God so loved the world that he gave his one and only Son, that whoever believes in him shall not perish but have eternal life" (John 3:16).

Help children learn the verse by using the hand motions as explained in session 2.

ACTIVITIES

Choose one or more of the following activities to support the story or theme and to provide a springboard for discussion.

TRIANGLE STARS. Cut pieces of paper into triangles with each side about 4 inches long. Give each person two triangles. Show how to place one triangle on top of the other so that the angles from the bottom triangle stick out from behind the top triangle to form a star of David. Color these, spread glue and glitter on them, or decorate them in other ways.

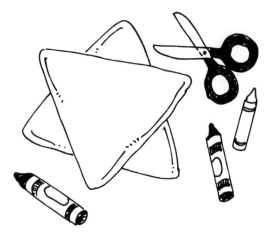

WINTER STARS. If the night is clear, take binoculars outside and look at the stars. Look for "shooting stars" or meteors that are common this time of year. While sitting under the stars, read Luke 2:1-20 and Matthew 2:1-12.

PRETZEL CAMELS. Let everyone glue pretzels (traditional pretzel shape, not sticks) onto paper. The two humps of the pretzel should be up. Draw a camel head and legs onto the pretzel body.

PIN THE BOW ON THE GIFT. Cut a section of gift-wrapping paper about 12 by 18 inches. Tape it to a wall or door. Give each person a bow that sticks on. Place a blindfold on one person at a time, turn him around, and head him toward the paper. He is to pin the bow on the gift (like the game Pin the Tail on the Donkey). Talk about how the leaders and teachers seemed to be blind and could not see that God had sent his Son. Also talk about what a gift Jesus was from the Father.

GIFT SEARCH. Hide a special treat or gift for everyone in the place where you keep your trash can, in the garden in a dirty spot, or in a box under a nativity scene. Make clues on numbered index cards that tell people where to look. The first clue cards tell them to look special places (under the Christmas tree, by the candles, on the wreath). At each place, searchers pick up another card that guides them somewhere else until they've found the gift. Discuss how, just as our gift was not hidden in one of the exciting places, the Son of God, our best gift, was not born in a castle or rich man's house but in a lowly stable.

QUESTIONS

1. Why did the wise men travel so far to see Jesus? Why did they bring him gifts?
2. Why would we consider Jesus to be a gift to us? How can we thank the one who gave us this gift?

KIDS' COUNCIL

BRING IT HOME
- Whom do you know who doesn't know about Jesus, God's gift?
- How can you share this gift with them?
- Is there anything we can give to God?
- How can you give to God this week?

SHARE AND PRAY
- Encourage the children to pray for each other.
- Thank God for sending Jesus.
- Pray for the people the children mentioned above.
- Pray for opportunity and courage to share the news of John 3:16.

ADULT STUDY QUESTIONS
- Compare the reactions of these three to the birth of Jesus: King Herod, the chief priests and teachers of the law, and the wise men. How do these reactions compare to the responses of people today to God's good news?
- The wise men were looking for a baby king. Jesus was to come from the lineage of King David. Read the genealogy of Jesus in Matthew 1. Tell what you know about some of the names listed there. (You can find their names in a concordance and read their stories in the Old Testament if you wish.) What does this tell us about God?
- Gold is a gift for a king. Incense represents a priest. Myrrh was a spice used for embalming, so it represents Jesus' death. Tell what Jesus as king means to you. How is Jesus a priest? (See Hebrews 7:23-28.) What does Jesus' death mean to you?

SNACK AND FELLOWSHIP

Cinnamon Stars. Make these ahead of time, or use them as an activity for children to make and share at snack time. Give each child one roll of canned, refrigerated Danish roll dough. Show them how to unroll it to its full length. Cut each long piece of dough in half. Form two triangles, one from each half. Put one triangle on top of the other so the angles of the bottom triangle show between the angles of the top triangle (a star of David). Bake by package directions. After frosting the stars, children may sprinkle them with cake decorations.

SESSION 4

Recognizing Jesus

OBJECTIVE: *To encourage each other to live in such a way that people can recognize Jesus living in us.*

■ ■ ■

WORSHIP

Sing songs about Jesus that are familiar and meaningful to your group. Here are some suggestions.
"Come Into His Presence"
"Fairest Lord Jesus"
"Hallelu, Hallelu"
"I Will Sing of the Mercies of the Lord"
"Jesus, Name Above All Names"
"We Bow Down"
"What a Mighty God We Serve"

STORY

Anna and Simeon See Baby Jesus in the Temple, Luke 2:21-40
- ■ Mary and Joseph take baby Jesus to the temple in Jerusalem.
- ■ Simeon sees the baby and praises God.
- ■ Anna sees the baby and thanks God.

Before group time, ask the oldest man in your group to play Simeon and the oldest woman to play Anna. They should read the Scripture and be familiar with what it says. At story time, you will pretend to be a TV interviewer. You will tell the "viewing audience" about Simeon and Anna. Then you will interview each of them. Ask each to read aloud from the Bible what they said when they saw Jesus.

MEMORY VERSE

"For God so loved the world that he gave his one and only Son, that whoever believes in him shall not perish but have eternal life" (John 3:16).

Help children learn the verse by using the hand motions suggested in session 2.

ACTIVITIES

Choose one or more of the following activities to support the story or theme and to provide a springboard for discussion.

TELESCOPES. Make pretend telescopes out of cardboard tubes from gift-wrapping paper or paper towels. Color them with markers. If you have a recording or lyrics to the song "Do You Hear What I Hear?," play it. Talk about who saw and recognized Jesus as the Son of God.

RIDDLE-MA-REE. Do you see what I see? Play a guessing game. One person chooses an object everyone can see and gives clues about it, saying, "Riddle-ma-riddle-ma-riddle-ma-ree. I see something you don't see. It is *(name of color)* and starts with a *(name of beginning letter)*." Discuss how the teachers and leaders did not see that the Messiah had come, but shepherds, the wise men, Mary, Joseph, Anna and Simeon saw.

WHO IS IT? Before your group meets, ask each person to bring a photograph of himself as a baby. Collect the photographs in a bag or basket as each person arrives so that no one else sees the photos. Then display the photographs on a table and let everyone see if they can identify each baby picture.

EARS. For younger children, show pictures of animals from a book or magazine, but cover up all of the animal except the ears. See if children can recognize the animal by looking only at the ears. Talk about the people who recognized Jesus as God's Son.

QUESTIONS

1. Who knew that Jesus was the Son of God? How did they know?
2. Why did the teachers and leaders not know?
3. Read Luke 2:25-35. Simeon knew a lot about this baby. What did he know? How do you think he knew that?
4. Read Luke 2:36-38. What did Anna do every day? What did she do when she saw baby Jesus?
5. What does God want us to do when we recognize Jesus as his Son?

KIDS' COUNCIL

BRING IT HOME
- How can you help others see Jesus?
- What does it mean to have Jesus living in you?
- Can people see Jesus living in you? How?
- How will people see Jesus in you this week?

SHARE AND PRAY
- Ask children to share their concerns and pray for each other.
- Pray that others will recognize Jesus living in us.
- Thank God for sending his only Son so we can have eternal life.

ADULT STUDY QUESTIONS
- What was Simeon's response when he recognized that this baby was God's Son? What was Anna's response? What does God want our response to be when we realize that we have met Jesus?
- Billy Graham said, "The greatest hindrance to Christianity today is Christians who do not know how to practice the presence of God" (*Engage,* Vol. 4, No. 4, Fall 1997).
  Is it possible not to recognize God or Jesus at work today? If so, how could that happen?
- What does it mean to have Jesus living in us? Tell about someone in whom you can recognize Jesus.

SNACK AND FELLOWSHIP

Covered Cookies. Use chocolate wafer cookies, vanilla wafers, or thin lemon flavored wafer cookies and whipped cream. Stack a cookie, then cream, then a cookie, then cream, and so on until the stack is tall. Lay the stack on its side and cover it all around with whipped cream so that it looks like a log. Chill the cookie log. Before you serve the log, ask if anyone knows what's inside. To serve it, cut it into sections. Now ask if people recognize what's inside. How do people see Jesus in us?

SESSION 5

Obedience

OBJECTIVE: *To choose ways in which we can obey and honor our parents.*

■ ■ ■

WORSHIP

Sing praise and worship songs as well as songs about obedience that are familiar and meaningful to your group. Here are some suggestions.

"Oh, Be Careful, Little Eyes"
"Change My Heart, O God"
"Freely, Freely"
"This Little Light of Mine"
"Trust and Obey"
"We Will Glorify"
"You Have Called Us"

STORY

Jesus Visits the Temple, Luke 2:41-52
- Twelve-year-old Jesus goes to Jerusalem with Mary and Joseph.
- Mary and Joseph search for Jesus after realizing he is not with them on the return trip.
- Mary and Joseph find Jesus in the temple.

As you tell the story, tape two pieces of plain white paper together at the narrow end. Fold them together and cut a diagonal line as shown. Now fold it accordion style and cut out the section indicated in the illustration. When you talk about Mary and Joseph finding Jesus in the temple, open the paper and show the temple you've cut out.

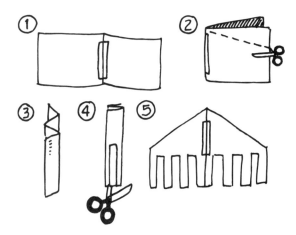

MEMORY VERSE

"Children, obey your parents in the Lord, for this is right" (Ephesians 6:1).

Help the children remember this verse by playing a game. Seat everyone in a circle. Everyone should pat their lap once with both hands, then clap once, then pat again and clap again. Establish a pattern: pat, clap, pat, clap. One person starts the game by saying the verse in rhythm. Then that person calls out another person's name. Everyone keeps up the clapping rhythm as the next person says the verse and calls out another person's name. Keep going until everyone has had a chance to say the verse. Pat on the italicized syllables and clap on the syllables in bold type.

"*Chil*dren, o**bey** your *par*ents **in** the *Lord*,
for **this** is *right*." E**phe**sians 6:**1**

ACTIVITIES

Choose one or more of the following activities to support the story or theme and to provide a springboard for discussion.

TISSUE CORSAGE. Give each person two facial tissues, laying one on top of the other. Set a small plate or saucer on top and trace around it to make a circle pattern. Cut out the circle through all layers of tissue. In the center of the circle, grasp about 1 inch of tissue through all layers. Tie a twist tie or pipe cleaner around it to secure it. This becomes the underside of the flower. Now separate the layers of each tissue, making petals. Spray cologne on it if you wish. Give these to moms. Read Ephesians 6:1, 2. Discuss honoring parents.

PAPER TOWEL RELAY. Divide into two teams. Each team lines up, one child behind another. Give each player two large paper towels. Mark a starting line and a turning point some distance away. When you say "Go," the first one on each team lays one paper towel on the ground in front of him and steps onto it. Then he lays the next paper towel down and steps onto it, and picks up the first paper towel. He lays that down, steps onto it, and picks up the paper towel that he just stepped off of. He continues this way until he reaches the turning point, where he picks up both paper towels and runs back to his team. Then it's the next player's turn to travel to the turning point and back. Say: "Sometimes we can honor someone by serving them, by helping. How do paper towels help us serve? How can we help/honor our parents?"

PLACE MATS. Each person gets two 18-inch lengths of waxed paper for each place mat he will make. Lay one piece flat on an ironing board. Cut out a paper heart and place it on top. Using a pencil sharpener, sharpen crayons of different colors so the shavings fall onto the waxed paper. Place the other piece of waxed paper on top. Iron it on a low heat setting to melt the crayon shavings and waxed paper together. Use these as gifts for parents.

LOOKING FOR SOMEONE. Seat everyone in a circle with enough chairs for every player except one. One player stands in the center. That player says, "I'm looking for someone who _____." He fills in the blank with almost anything, such as "is wearing blue," "plays baseball," "is over ten years old," or "has been to Disney World." All people who fit the description must change seats. The player in the center tries to sit in a vacant seat before someone else gets to it. The person left standing says, "I'm looking for someone who _____," and the game continues. Talk about Mary and Joseph looking for Jesus.

QUESTIONS

1. What does it mean to honor someone? Is it always easy to honor others? Why or why not? Tell about someone you know who honors others—what do they do?
2. Read Philippians 2:3, 4. What does it mean? How can you look "to the interests of others"?

KIDS' COUNCIL

BRING IT HOME
- Read Ephesians 6:2, 3. Whom does it tell us to honor?
- How can we honor our parents? Why is it important to honor our mothers and fathers?
- How will you honor your parents this week?

SHARE AND PRAY
- Encourage children to share concerns and pray for each other.
- Ask children to pray for their parents.
- Pray for God to help children honor their parents.

ADULT STUDY QUESTIONS
- What was Jesus doing in the temple courts? Why do you think his parents were astonished?
- What did Mary say to Jesus? What did he answer? Why do you think Joseph and Mary didn't understand what he was saying?
- Should we as adults honor our parents? Is it easy or difficult to honor your parents? Why?
- How can we as adults honor our parents?

SNACK AND FELLOWSHIP

Apple Cinnamon Muffins. Mix together:

1 ½ cups flour	½ cup wheat germ
¼ cup sugar	1 tablespoon baking powder
1 teaspoon cinnamon	½ teaspoon salt

In another bowl, mix:

1 cup of milk	3 tablespoons vegetable oil
2 lightly beaten egg whites	1 cup chopped apple

Add the apple mixture to the flour mixture and stir it until moistened. Fill twelve greased muffin cups. Mix 1 tablespoon sugar and ¼ teaspoon cinnamon. Sprinkle the mixture on muffins. Bake 20 minutes at 400 degrees. Ask the children to serve the muffins to their parents to honor them.

SESSION 6

Who Is Jesus?

OBJECTIVE: *To explore the character of Jesus and the hope he gives us.*

■ ■ ■

WORSHIP

Sing praise and worship songs as well as songs about Jesus that are familiar and meaningful to your group. Here are some suggestions.
- "Fairest Lord Jesus"
- "Jesus in the Morning"
- "Jesus Is All the World to Me"
- "Jesus, Mighty God"
- "Jesus, Name Above All Names"
- "O How I Love Jesus"
- "Praise the Name of Jesus"

STORY

Jesus' Baptism, Matthew 3:13-17; John 1:29-34
- ■ Jesus is baptized by John in the Jordan River.
- ■ The Holy Spirit comes in the form of a dove, and God says, "This is my Son."
- ■ Later, John tells what has happened.

Fold a blue sheet in half lengthwise and stretch it across the floor or grass. Pretend it's the river. Everyone gathers there, sitting beside the "river" while you read or tell the story.

Option: Go to a creek or sit by a swimming pool while you tell the story.

MEMORY VERSE

"I have seen and I testify that this is the Son of God" (John 1:34).

Discuss the meaning of the word *testify*. Help the children remember the verse by singing it to the tune of "Mary Had a Little Lamb."

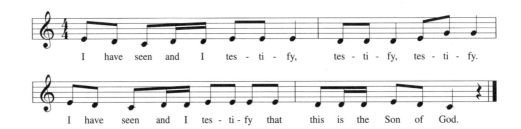

ACTIVITIES

Choose one or more of the following activities to support the story or theme and to provide a springboard for discussion.

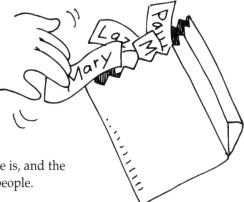

CLUES. Cut slips of paper about 2 by 3 inches. On each, write the name of a famous Bible character Jesus knew, helped, or talked about (Peter, the Good Samaritan, Mary or Martha, Lazarus, John the Baptist, blind Bartimaeus). Each person draws a slip of paper from a hat or bag. Sit in a circle. Each person gives clues about who he is, and the others guess. Talk about how Jesus affected each of these people.

NAMES. Divide everyone into four groups. Assign each group one name of Jesus from Isaiah 9:6—Wonderful Counselor, Mighty God, Everlasting Father, Prince of Peace. Give groups old magazines and scissors and tell them to cut out the letters that spell that name. Then they glue the letters to paper, spelling their assigned name. Discuss how Jesus fulfills each of those names.

PAPER CHAIN. Make a paper chain by cutting colored construction paper into 1-inch-wide strips. On each strip, people write a name of Jesus (see above; let them suggest others: Good Shepherd, Living Word, God's Son, Messiah, Christ). Link strips together by making each into a ring looped through another ring. Tape or staple in place.

PAPER PLATE MASKS. Make paper plate masks, using large paper plates and crayons. Cut holes for eyes. Punch holes in the sides and tie string there. Let children model the masks for the adults. The adults guess who is behind the mask. Talk about ways we recognize people. If we saw a plate of cookies in the kitchen, we might say, "Mom has been at work here." Discuss how we recognize Jesus at work around us.

QUESTIONS

1. What is Jesus like?
2. What did he do here on earth?
3. How did people find out about Jesus? Did he advertise?
4. Has Jesus changed?
5. Why are you thankful for Jesus?

KIDS' COUNCIL

BRING IT HOME
- What is hope?
- How is hope different than wishes?
- How does Jesus give people hope?
- How can you testify and share your hope with people?
- Who can you share your hope with?
  (You may want to use this lesson as an opportunity to discuss baptism with children.)

SHARE AND PRAY
- Ask children to share prayer needs and pray for each other.
- Thank Jesus for the hope he gives us.
- Thank God for the people who testified about Jesus to us, and ask him who he wants us to share our testimony with.

ADULT STUDY QUESTIONS
- What was the significance of Jesus' baptism to John? to Jesus? to God? to the people watching? to us?
- What is hope? How is it different than wishes?
- Read and discuss Hebrews 11:1. How are faith and hope related?
- Read and discuss Romans 15:13.

SNACK AND FELLOWSHIP
Ask someone to bring his favorite brand of cookies or crackers. Before eating, ask that person to testify about the quality of the cookies or crackers he has chosen. Then let others try it and see if they agree or disagree. Ask: "When we testify about Jesus, does everyone agree with us?"

SESSION 7

Temptation and the Choices We Make

OBJECTIVE: *To learn why and how to fight temptation and to encourage each other to fight temptation.*

■ ■ ■

WORSHIP

Sing praise and worship songs as well as songs about temptation and choices that are familiar and meaningful to your group. Here are some suggestions.

"Oh, Be Careful, Little Eyes"
"Greater Is He That Is in Me"
"I Need Thee Every Hour"
"I Will Call Upon the Lord"
"I'm in the Lord's Army"
"Into My Heart"
"The Battle Belongs to the Lord"

STORY

Jesus Is Tempted in the Desert, Matthew 4:1-11
- ■ Jesus goes to the desert and does not eat for forty days and nights.
- ■ Satan tempts Jesus three times, and Jesus resists.
- ■ Angels take care of Jesus.

Hold up a calendar to show how long forty days are. Set out a loaf of bread as you tell about the first temptation. Ask a small child to stand on a chair as you tell about the temptation to jump off the temple. Let a man hold a small child on his shoulders as you tell about Jesus surveying the earth and being tempted to worship the devil.

MEMORY VERSE

"Do not follow the crowd in doing wrong" (Exodus 23:2).

To help the children remember the verse, play a following game. Form a single line, one person behind the other. The first person leads the others in a circle. Everyone must follow his movements as in "Follow the Leader." But as they march, the last person says the verse, "Do not follow the crowd in doing wrong." Then he taps the person in front of him and stands still while the rest of the line keeps going. The person who is now last in line says the verse, taps the person in front of him and stands still. This continues as the line gets smaller, still moving around the circle, but now weaving in and out of the people who are standing still. When everyone has said the verse, the game is over.

ACTIVITIES

Choose one or more of the following activities to support the story or theme and to provide a springboard for discussion.

COLORED GLASSES. Cut paper plates in half. Make half-masks by cutting eye holes in them and tying string to the sides. Tape colored cellophane over the eye holes. Read the memory verse and discuss seeing things differently than the way the world sees them.

LIFESTYLES. Let everyone look through magazines that show lifestyles of rich and famous people, or tell about rich and famous people they've heard about. Talk about envy. Ask: "Do riches make people happy? Does fame make people happy? Why does this tempt us?"

INSIDE ME. Give each person a paper lunch sack. Draw a large circle on the front. Let each person draw a face in the circle to represent himself. He may glue on yarn or construction paper hair. Inside the sack, place things that will fill us with joy: a red paper heart (love), a small piece of black paper folded in half (God's Word), an index card with Jesus on it, the person's handprint traced on paper. Say: "These represent some of the most important things in the world. Think about how Jesus answered when he was tempted. What do you think was important to him? How does knowing what's important to us help when we're tempted?"

HIKING. Take a compass along as you hike around the neighborhood. Stop once in awhile to check the compass and see which direction you are going. Talk about other ways to tell direction (movement of sun, stars, and so on). Talk about how we can be like a compass, pointing out the right way to each other when we have to make decisions in school and at home. Ask: "What did Jesus choose? How can we know what's right?" Discuss Psalm 119:105 and Hebrews 10:24.

BACKWARDS RELAY. Form two teams. Mark a start and turn-around line. When you say go, the first player on each team walks backwards to the turn line, then walks backwards to his team. Each player in line does the same. The team finishing first wins. Talk about how we do things in a way that looks backwards to the world. Say: "When the world hates, we love. When the world lies and cheats, we're honest. Why be different?"

QUESTIONS

1. What is temptation?
2. How can we overcome temptation? How did Jesus do it?
3. How is God's Word like a light on a pathway?
4. Why is the way we act important?
5. How do we know the right way to act? Is it easy to choose the right way? Tell of a time when it would be hard.

KIDS' COUNCIL

BRING IT HOME
- Can we encourage each other to do right? How?
- Can we encourage each other to do wrong? How?
- If someone is encouraging us to do wrong, what should we do?
- Tell of a time when someone you know encouraged another person to do right. What happened?

SHARE AND PRAY
- Ask children to share their concerns and pray for each other.
- Pray for God's help in recognizing and fighting temptation.
- Pray that they will be brave enough to go against the crowd when the crowd is choosing wrong.
- Pray as Jesus did, "Lead us not into temptation" (Matthew 6:13).

ADULT STUDY QUESTIONS
- Read and discuss 1 John 2:15-17 as it relates to temptation.
- How did Jesus fight temptation? If he is our example, how does that mean we should fight temptation?
- Think of something that tempts you. What Scripture can you quote the next time this temptation comes your way? (You may need concordances to answer this question.)

SNACK AND FELLOWSHIP
Fish Crackers in Soup. Heat a pan of soup or tomato/vegetable juice. Let everyone drop fish-shaped crackers into it. Then ask them to watch as you pour the soup into cups. Ask: "Where do the fish go? When water is flowing down a river, which direction do fish usually swim? Do they ever swim upstream? Which would be harder—to swim upstream or downstream? Why? Sometimes when we don't follow the crowd, it is like swimming upstream."

SESSION 8

Jesus Calls His Disciples

OBJECTIVE: *To contemplate Jesus' role as our Lord and learn from him how to be a good leader as well as a good disciple.*

■ ■ ■

WORSHIP

Sing praise and worship songs as well as songs about following Jesus that are familiar and meaningful to your group. Here are some suggestions.

"I Have Decided to Follow Jesus"
"I'm in the Lord's Army"
"Jesus Called Them One by One"
"Jesus Loves Even Me"
"O How I Love Jesus"
"Savior, Like a Shepherd Lead Us"
"You Have Called Us"

STORY

Jesus Calls His Disciples, Matthew 4:18-22; John 1:43-49; Matthew 9:9

■ Jesus asks four fishermen to follow him.
■ Philip and Nathanael follow Jesus.
■ Jesus asks a tax collector to follow him.

Before you gather, look up passages in the Bible about each apostle (or ask older children to do this for you). A concordance will help. Find a few facts about each apostle. There will be more information on some of them than others. As you read the story to the group, tell about each disciple. Then ask children to tell what they think they might have smelled, heard, seen, and felt if they had been there with Jesus. Ask what they might have felt like if they had been the ones Jesus called.

MEMORY VERSE

"Obey your leaders and submit to their authority" (Hebrews 13:17).

Discuss the meaning of the words *submit* and *authority*. Then, to help the children learn this verse, sing it to the tune of "The Old Gray Mare" (page 40).

38

ACTIVITIES

Choose one or more of the following activities to support the story or theme and to provide a springboard for discussion.

ADD-ON TAG. Choose a leader. He tries to tag the other players. The first one tagged must hold onto the leader's waist and follow him around. The second tagged holds onto the first one and so on, forming a line that follows the leader. Both the leader and the person at the end of the line may tag. They may also tag people by making the line into a circle that surrounds a person. The last person tagged becomes the next leader. Discuss lordship and leadership.

HIDE A HEART. Cut a heart shape out of paper. In the room where you will do this activity, place a Bible and some objects (toys, a TV set, magazines, a piggy bank, food). Choose one person to be IT. He closes his eyes. Another person hides the paper heart. The first person tries to find it. Ask: "Where is your heart?" Discuss different places people could "put their hearts" with money, food, and so on.

FOLLOWING. Method 1: The adult leader describes (only once) to the children a path to follow around the yard or in the house. Make it fairly complex: around the swing set two times, up the slide, around the house, up and down the driveway, and so on. Children try to follow the directions. Method 2: The leader walks the path first. Children watch and then run the path. Ask: "Is it easier to follow the path?" Method 3: Children follow the leader as he runs the path. Ask: "Is it easier to stay on course?" Discuss the difference between these three methods. Ask: "Which is easiest? What did Jesus do for his disciples (us)?"

WHO'S THE LEADER? Everyone sits in a circle. One person who is chosen to be IT is out of the room. A leader is chosen from among the others. IT returns. The leader, trying not to be obvious, begins a movement (scratching, tapping) and everyone in the circle copies that movement until the leader changes the movement, which they also copy. The trick is to do it so smoothly that IT has to work to figure out who is the leader. IT has three guesses, and then the leader chooses a new IT. IT becomes the new leader. Discuss leaders and the word *disciple*. Read and discuss Exodus 23:2, "Do not follow the crowd in doing wrong."

QUESTIONS

1. What is a leader? Why do we need leaders?
2. What is a disciple? Can you be a disciple of Jesus?
3. Did everyone like the followers of Jesus? Does everyone like followers of Jesus today? What happens sometimes between Jesus' followers and people who are not followers of Jesus?

KIDS' COUNCIL
BRING IT HOME
- What does a good leader do? What does a bad leader do? What is a lord? Who is our Lord? What makes him Lord? How can he become Lord of your life? What does that mean? Read Hebrews 13:17. Discuss who else might be our leader or authority under Jesus' authority.
- From the word *disciple* we get the word *discipline*. What does discipline have to do with being a follower of Jesus? Are there things we may have to give up to be a disciple of Jesus?
- Are there rewards for making Jesus the Lord of your life? What are they?
  (This is a good opportunity to ask the children if they want to ask Jesus to be Lord of their lives and to discuss how to be his followers.)

SHARE AND PRAY
- Ask children to share their concerns and pray for each other.
- Pray that when they are chosen to lead, they will be good leaders.
- Pray that God will give them good leaders and thank God for some of the good leaders in their lives.

ADULT STUDY QUESTIONS
- Read Matthew 16:24-26. What does this mean to you today? Compare this to Matthew 11:29, 30.
- From the word *disciple* we get the word *discipline*. What does discipline have to do with being a follower of Jesus? What are some spiritual disciplines that we practice as disciples of Jesus, and why are they important in our time?
- List some qualities you think are important in a good leader. Name someone you consider to be a good leader. Tell why you think that person is a good leader.

SNACK AND FELLOWSHIP

Healthy Muffins. Pour ½ cup of boiling water over 1 cup bran flakes or All Bran cereal. Add ½ cup cooking oil. Mix in:

1 cup oats	½ pound brown sugar
1 cup wheat germ	2 cups buttermilk
2 ½ cups flour	2 ½ teaspoons soda
½ teaspoon salt	2 eggs, beaten

Bake in greased muffin tins for 15-20 minutes at 400 degrees. This batter can be refrigerated and used up to a month later. Ask: "What would happen if you did not follow the recipe? What would happen if you put in ½ pound of soda instead of brown sugar? What happens to people when they choose not to follow Jesus?"

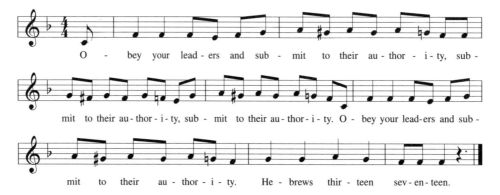

SESSION 9

Revival, the Waking Up

OBJECTIVE: *To learn what revival is and why we need it.*

■ ■ ■

WORSHIP

Sing praise and worship songs as well as songs about the heart that are familiar and meaningful to your group. Here are some suggestions.

"As a Deer"
"Deep and Wide"
"Down in My Heart"
"Kum Ba Yah"

"Lord, You're Beautiful"
"My Life Is in You, Lord"
"Revive Us Again"
"Standin' in the Need of Prayer"

STORY

Jesus at the Wedding in Cana, John 2:1-11

■ Jesus goes to a wedding.
■ Mary tells Jesus that they've run out of wine.
■ Jesus turns water into wine.

Give each person an empty cup. In the bottom of an empty, dry pitcher, sprinkle a package of grape pre-sweetened powdered drink mix. Tell the story, and at the right time, pour clear water into the pitcher. Gently swirl the pitcher as you talk. Then pour the drink into each person's cup and let them all drink it.

MEMORY VERSE

"I live in a high and holy place, but also with him who is contrite and lowly in spirit to revive the spirit of the lowly and to revive the heart of the contrite" (Isaiah 57:15).

Make sure that the children know that the *I* in this verse is God. Talk about the meaning of these words: *Revive* means to bring back to life or to make something useful again. *Contrite* means to be sorry for the wrong that's been done. *Lowly* means not bragging or boastful, taking the place of a servant or helper.

To help the children learn this verse, put hand motions to it.

I live in a high and holy place (both arms stretched up)
but also with him who is contrite (right fist over heart)
and lowly in spirit (left fist over heart)
to revive the spirit of the lowly (open and extend left hand)
and to revive the heart of the contrite (open and extend right hand)

ACTIVITIES

Choose one or more of the following activities to support the story or theme and to provide a springboard for discussion.

FIREWORKS PICTURE. On plain white paper, each person colors a design with a variety of colors. Over this, they color heavily with a black crayon. Give each person a toothpick and show them how to scratch through the black in a design that looks like spokes of a wheel to make fireworks, revealing the color underneath. Talk about spiritual revival putting the excitement back into life. Ask: "How did Jesus revive the wedding? What is exciting about being Jesus' friend, being God's child?"

CPR. If you have someone in your group who knows CPR, let him tell everyone about how he would go about reviving someone. Talk about why a person would need to be revived. Ask: "What is spiritual revival? Why would people need it?"

ENERGY. Play a game outside (tag, jump rope, relays, kickball, softball, basketball) until everyone is hot and tired. Serve cold drinks and talk about how it revives us. Ask: "Why do we need to be revived? How? Why do people need spiritual revival? How does that happen?"

REVIVING THE TEA. Make a weak mixture of instant unsweetened tea in lukewarm water. Let everyone drink a little of it. Now suggest that you "revive" this drink. Add more tea, lemon juice and sugar (or simply mix lemonade with it). Serve over ice. Add a sprig of mint. Ask: "What did Jesus revive at the wedding?" Talk about what revival is. Ask: "What is a spiritual revival?" Talk about lukewarm lives.

QUESTIONS

1. What is revival? Compare physical revival and spiritual revival.
2. Who needs to be revived spiritually? Why? Do you ever need it?
3. If you know of someone who has been revived (physically or spiritually), tell about it.

KIDS' COUNCIL

BRING IT HOME
- Read Isaiah 57:15. Talk about what it means to be contrite and lowly. Why will these people be revived?
- Do you ever need to be revived in your spirit?
- Do you know of someone else who needs to be revived? How can you help them this week?
- If everyone at church was revived, what do you think your church meetings would be like?

SHARE AND PRAY
- Ask children to share their concerns and pray for each other.
- Pray for God to revive them, to give them new energy in their spirits when they pray and worship.
- Pray for God to revive his people all over the world.

ADULT STUDY QUESTIONS
- How does spiritual revival happen? When does it happen? What is true revival?
- Do you need to be revived in any way: physically, mentally, emotionally?
- What could God do to revive you spiritually? What can you do to help God revive you?
- Would your church meetings be any different if everyone was revived spiritually? If so, how would your meetings be different?
- Is revival necessary? Why or why not?

SNACK AND FELLOWSHIP

Popcorn Pizzazz. Pop plain popcorn to fill a big bowl. Set out a variety of toppings: salt, pepper, melted butter or margarine, grated cheeses, basil, cinnamon and sugar, caramel sauce. Give each person a bowl and let him make his own flavor of popcorn. Talk about reviving things that are bland: foods, a room, a relationship, spiritual life.

SESSION 10

Knowing Jesus

OBJECTIVE: *To recognize that only Jesus can satisfy us and to encourage each other to get to know him better.*

■ ■ ■

WORSHIP

Sing praise and worship songs as well as songs about Jesus that are familiar and meaningful to your group. Here are some suggestions.

"As a Deer"
"Fairest Lord Jesus"
"God With Us"
"Jesus Is All the World to Me"
"Jesus Loves Me"
"Jesus in the Morning"
"Jesus, Name Above All Names"
"No, Not One!"
"O How I Love Jesus"
"What a Friend We Have in Jesus"

STORY

Nicodemus, John 3:1-20

■ Nicodemus visits Jesus at night.
■ Jesus tells Nicodemus what he must do to enter God's kingdom.
■ Jesus tells Nicodemus why God sent his Son.

Turn off the lights and read the story by lamplight or flashlight.

MEMORY VERSE

"He [Jesus] is the image of the invisible God" (Colossians 1:15).

To help the children learn the verse, write it backwards on a piece of paper. Let the children hold it in front of a mirror to see its image reversed and read the verse. Talk about what it means for Jesus to be the image of the invisible God.

44

ACTIVITIES

Choose one or more of the following activities to support the story or theme and to provide a springboard for discussion.

WHAT'S INSIDE? Show a glove, an uninflated balloon, and a flashlight without batteries. Ask what should fill these so they can do what they were made to do. Let a child put on the glove, blow up the balloon, and put batteries in the flashlight. Ask what we need to fill us so we can do what we were made to do (God's Holy Spirit). Ask: "What were we made to do?" (See Ephesians 2:10.)

WHO KNEW JESUS? If your group knows lots of Bible stories, write on index cards names of people who knew Jesus. (For example: Mary and Martha, Lazarus, Peter, Zacchaeus.) Each person draws a card and tells what that person might tell you about Jesus. Discuss Philippians 3:8 and what it means to know Jesus.

JARS OF CLAY. Each person makes a jar or bowl from play dough (3 parts flour, 1 part salt, 1 part water). Each person tells what he would put in his jar or bowl. Talk about God as our potter and people as the clay (Isaiah 64:8). Say: "God wants to fill us with his Spirit."

BALL GAME. Play kickball or softball. Make the playing field heart-shaped. Each base represents something with which a person could try to fill their lives. First base represents money. Second is entertainment. Third is friends and family. Home base represents Jesus. Ask: "Which fills a person's heart?"

QUESTIONS

1. How do you get to know a person?
2. How do you get to know Jesus?
3. How can you introduce someone else to Jesus?
4. What do you like best about Jesus? What's your favorite part about being in God's kingdom?

KIDS' COUNCIL

BRING IT HOME

- What do people try to fill their lives with? (Or to satisfy the empty feeling inside?) Do these things work?
- What is the only thing that will fill us so we are satisfied, at peace, and happy?
- How can you get to know Jesus better this week?
- How can you help someone else know Jesus better this week?

SHARE AND PRAY

- Ask children to share their concerns and pray for each other.
- Thank God for sending Jesus to show us what he is like.
- Pray for Jesus to help them know him better.

ADULT STUDY QUESTIONS

- What does it mean to be born again? With the John 3 passage in mind, read 1 Peter 1:3-5, 22-25; James 1:18; Titus 3:4-7; Romans 6:1-11; 2 Corinthians 5:17; Ephesians 4:22-24; Matthew 18:3. Discuss being born again in light of these passages.
- Is there a difference in knowing about Jesus and knowing Jesus? If so, what's the difference?
- Some people describe wanting to know Jesus better as being hungry or thirsty (Psalm 63:1-4; 42:1, 2). What do they mean? Have you ever felt this way? What "feeds" you?
- How does a person get to know Jesus?

SNACK AND FELLOWSHIP

Cinnamon Spice Tea. Blend two 9-ounce packages of red hots in a blender or food processor until they are powdered. Mix :

1 large jar of orange breakfast drink mix	1 cup of brown sugar
1¼ teaspoons of cinnamon	powdered red hots
1⅓ cups of instant tea	1 large package of lemonade mix

For each serving, put 2 to 3 heaping teaspoons of this mix in a mug. Add 1 cup of hot water. For young children, let the hot tea cool or put an ice cube in it to cool it before they drink it. Talk about making special food and drinks for guests. Ask: "Do you think Jesus might have served Nicodemus something to eat or drink when he visited?"

SESSION 11

Worship and Praise

OBJECTIVE: *To learn what true worship is and encourage each other to worship.*

■ ■ ■

WORSHIP

Sing praise and worship songs that are familiar and meaningful to your group. Here are some suggestions.

"Be Exalted, O God"
"Clap Your Hands"
"Come Let Us Worship and Bow Down"
"Father, I Adore You"
"Great Is the Lord"
"Holy, Holy, Holy"
"How Great Thou Art"
"Let's Just Praise the Lord"

"O Worship the King"
"Praise Him, Praise Him"
"Praise the Name of Jesus"
"Thou Art Worthy"
"To God Be the Glory"
"We Bow Down"
"We Will Glorify"

STORY

The Woman at the Well, John 4:1-42

■   A woman comes to get water at a well where Jesus is resting.
■   Jesus asks the woman for a drink.
■   Jesus talks to the woman about worship and reveals who he is.

Make a pretend well: Place four chairs in a circle, or place pillows and cushions on top of each other in a circle, or use a large, empty box to make a well. Tie a string or rope to a bucket or small box. Let it down into the "well" as you tell the story.

MEMORY VERSE

"God is spirit, and his worshipers must worship in spirit and in truth" (John 4:24).

To help the children remember the verse, write the words of the verse on index cards, one word for each card. Line the cards up in order. Everyone reads the verse together. Ask one child to turn over any card he wants. Read the verse together again, saying the correct word that belongs on the card that is facedown. Ask another child to turn over another card. Read together again, supplying the missing words. Keep going like this until all cards are turned over and everyone is saying the verse by memory.

ACTIVITIES

Choose one or more of the following activities to support the story or theme and to provide a springboard for discussion.

WORSHIP INSTRUMENTS. Make instruments to use in your group worship. An empty margarine tub or oatmeal box with a lid can be a drum. Fill a margarine tub or empty soft drink can with dried beans or unpopped popcorn. Tape the lid on the tub, or tape over the opening of the can. This is a shaker. Building blocks or dowels can be tapped together as wood blocks. Pots and pans, with or without lids, can be instruments, struck with a wooden spoon. Now sing songs of praise and make a joyful noise.

WORSHIP. Have an extended worship time. Let the children choose and lead songs; let them pray and dance if they wish.

READ AND JUMP. Read Psalm 148. Give each person paper and crayons or markers. Tell each person the name of one thing this psalm tells to praise the Lord (angels, sun, moon, and so on). Tell each person more than one if you need to. The person then draws and colors that object. Now read the psalm. When a person hears the name of what he has drawn, he stands and holds up the picture. To make it more fun, go through the psalm as many times as you wish, speeding up each time, so everyone is popping up and down quickly, listening for the names of their pictures.

WORSHIP OUTSIDE. Sit outside and talk about how David often sat outside watching his sheep and talking to God in prayer or with psalms. Read Psalm 23, Psalm 8, and Psalm 19:1-6.

OUR PSALMS. Ask everyone to write their own psalms. If they have a hard time doing this individually, write psalms as a group, letting each person suggest a few lines.

PRAISE. For girls: Put lipstick on each girl's lips. Let each girl press her lips to a piece of plain white paper to make a lip print. At the bottom of the paper, write "His praise will always be on my lips" (Psalm 34:1). For boys: Give each boy a small plate with some dry powdered drink mix (like Kool-Aid) of a dark color sprinkled on it. He licks his lips to moisten them, then presses them onto the drink mix. Quickly wipe the paper with a damp cloth or sponge. He presses his lips to the paper. Write Psalm 34:1 on the paper.

QUESTIONS

1. What is worship? (Looking up to God, loving him, telling him we think he is the greatest.)
2. What is praise? (When we praise someone, we tell them they did good work, a great job. When we praise God, we tell him he is the best, the greatest, he has done wonderful things, we love him and thank him.)
3. When should we worship? Where can we worship? Is it done only when we get together on Sundays?
4. Can we worship when we are having a bad day, or when things are not going well?

KIDS' COUNCIL

BRING IT HOME
- How can we worship?
- What is your favorite way to worship?
- How will you worship every day this week?

SHARE AND PRAY
- Ask children to share their concerns and pray for each other.
- Pray a psalm by reading it prayerfully together.
- Ask children to tell God something that they think is wonderful about him.

ADULT STUDY QUESTIONS
- Is there a difference between praise and worship? If so, what is the difference?
- Why does God want us to praise and worship him?
- What did Jesus mean when he said that God's worshipers "must worship him in spirit and truth"?
- Read Romans 12:1. According to this verse, what is our spiritual worship? In practical terms, how can we do this?

SNACK AND FELLOWSHIP

Celebration Sundaes. Set out several small bowls of sundae toppings, including fudge and caramel sauce, assorted sprinkles, chopped nuts, crushed chocolate wafers, maraschino cherries, and whipped cream. Serve ice cream or frozen yogurt and let everyone add their own chosen toppings. Talk about how we sometimes celebrate special times with special treats like cakes and sundaes. Say: "We celebrate God's goodness and love by praising and worshiping him."

SESSION 12

Failure

OBJECTIVE: *To encourage each other to see failures as learning opportunities.*

■ ■ ■

WORSHIP

Sing praise and worship songs as well as songs about God's help that are familiar and meaningful to your group. Here are some suggestions.

"Amazing Grace"
"Do Lord"
"God Will Make a Way"
"It Is Well With My Soul"
"Kum Ba Yah"
"No, Not One!"
"O Most High"
"The Joy of the Lord"
"The Lord Is My Shepherd"
"Through It All"

STORY

The Great Catch of Fish, Luke 5:1-11
- ■ Jesus tells Peter to put out the nets to catch fish.
- ■ Peter protests but puts out the nets anyway.
- ■ They catch so many fish that they have to have help to bring them in.

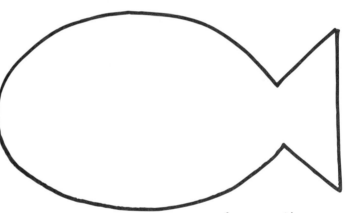

fish pattern

Cut fish out of paper or cardboard. You may use the pattern on this page. Scatter the fish around the floor or grass. Choose one person to work with the fish. Guide the others in pretending to cast a net (a sheet) out of their pretend boat (a couch or imaginary boat). The worker scoops up the fish and puts them on the net so the children can pull in the net full of fish.

MEMORY VERSE

"Though a righteous man falls seven times, he rises again" (Proverbs 24:16).

To help the children remember this verse, ask everyone to stand to begin saying the verse. Tell them to *squat* when they say the word *fall*. Tell them to stand up again when they say *rises again*. Say the verse several times with the actions.

ACTIVITIES

Choose one or more of the following activities to support the story or theme and to provide a springboard for discussion.

DOMINO TUMBLE. Divide everyone into two groups. Give each group a set, or half a set, of dominoes. Each group is to set up a domino tumble (a line of dominoes standing on end, one behind the other). The group that finishes first wins. Ask: "How do you feel when you lose? How do you feel if you are the one who knocks down your dominoes before the line is finished? How does failure make people feel?"

PACK SADDLE. Take "pack saddle" rides. Two bigger children or adults stand facing each other. Each of them places his right hand around his left forearm and his left hand on the right forearm of the other person. This forms the saddle. They stoop down to let a smaller child sit on this like a swing. Then they carry him across the room this way. Read Ecclesiastes 4:9, 10, "Two are better than one, because they have a good return for their work: If one falls down, his friend can help him up. But pity the man who falls and has no one to help him up!" Talk about how friends can encourage us when we have failed.

BADGES. Make badges that say "Under Construction." Ask: "Is anyone perfect?" Read Psalm 138:8, "The Lord will fulfill his purpose for me," and Philippians 1:6, "He who began a good work in you will carry it on to completion."

RING AROUND THE ROSY. Play the game. Every time the children fall down, they recite Proverbs 24:16, "Though a *righteous* man falls seven times, he rises again." Talk about what righteous means (right). Talk about how making mistakes is like falling—you try again.

QUESTIONS

1. How do you feel when you fail? Are you tempted to give up?
2. How can you encourage others?
3. How does God encourage us?

KIDS' COUNCIL

BRING IT HOME
- Talk about someone who encouraged you when you failed at something. How did he encourage you?
- What can you do when you are discouraged?
- Whom do you know who needs to be encouraged?
- How will you encourage that person this week?

SHARE AND PRAY
- Ask children to share their concerns and pray for each other.
- Thank God for giving us the skills and abilities we have.
- Ask God to encourage us when we fail.
- Ask God to teach us and bring something good out of our failures.

ADULT STUDY QUESTIONS
- How did your parents view failure? How do you view failure?
- Tell about a time when God brought something good out of a failure.
- Did Jesus ever fail? Explain.
- Do you feel like you've failed at anything recently? How are you handling your failure?

SNACK AND FELLOWSHIP
Heart Snacks. Use a can of refrigerated bread stick dough. Roll the dough into "snakes" and bend them into the outline of a heart. Bake according to package directions. Talk about how God will never stop loving us.

SESSION 13

Prayer, the Power Line

OBJECTIVE: *To recognize prayer as powerful communication and to commit to pray.*

■ ■ ■

WORSHIP

Sing praise and worship songs as well as songs about prayer that are familiar and meaningful to your group. Here are some suggestions.

"Dear Lord and Father of Mankind"
"God Is So Good"
"Standin' in the Need of Prayer"
"Whisper a Prayer"

STORY

Jesus Goes Out to Pray, Mark 1:35-37

■ Jesus goes out to pray alone, early in the morning.
■ Peter and the disciples look for Jesus.
■ The disciples tell Jesus that everyone is looking for him.

Dim the lights as if it's early morning. Let people in your group describe early morning outdoors. Then read the Scripture.

MEMORY VERSE

"In the morning, O Lord, you hear my voice; in the morning I lay my requests before you and wait in expectation" (Psalm 5:3).

To help the children learn the verse, show them some hand motions they can do as they say the verse.

In the morning, O Lord, (arms form a circle around the head)
you hear my voice; (point to the mouth)
in the morning (arms form a circle around the head again)
I lay my requests before you (hold hands out as if giving a gift)
and wait in expectation. (look up toward heaven)

ACTIVITIES

Choose one or more of the following activities to support the story or theme and to provide a springboard for discussion.

POWER LINE PICTURES. Each person glues a line of toothpicks in T shapes onto paper. Then he tapes or glues string between the Ts to form power lines. Write on the paper "Prayer is my Power Line." Ask: "Has the power ever gone off at your home? Why?" Discuss power lines and their importance in our daily lives. Discuss prayer as a power line. Ask: "What happens when we don't pray?" Talk about light versus darkness.

AIR POWER/PRAYER POWER. Demonstrate the power of air. Point the nozzle of a hair dryer upward. Place a Ping-Pong ball on it and turn it to low. Watch. Then turn it to high. Watch it for only a minute. Then turn it off to let it cool. Ask: "What happened to the ball when the dryer was on? Why? Can you see air (or wind)? Does it have power? Can you see prayers? Can you see God? What happens when you pray?" Read Psalm 34 and discuss prayer.

AIR POWER RELAY. Play this on a smooth, uncarpeted floor. Line up, one behind another, in two teams. Mark a starting line and a finish line some distance away. Give each person a cotton ball. The first person in each line places his cotton ball on the floor and gets down on hands and knees behind it. When you say "Go," the first on each team blows his cotton ball to the finish line, then the next team member goes. The first team to get everyone over the finish line wins. Discuss questions from the previous activity.

PRAYER PULLEY. On paper, trace each person's hand (fingers together as in prayer) and cut it out. Tape or staple each hand to an 8-foot length of string. Let each person draw or write some of God's blessings on index cards or small pieces of paper. Attach these to the other end of his string. Two people hold a broom handle horizontally between them. Each person drapes his string over the handle so the hands are near the floor. Sing the third verse of "The Wise Man and the Foolish Man" as each person pulls the blessing end of the string to raise up the hands.

> So build your life on the Lord Jesus Christ.
> Build your life on the Lord Jesus Christ.
> Build your life on the Lord Jesus Christ,
> And the blessings will come down.
> The blessings come down as the prayers go up.
> The blessings come down as the prayers go up.
> The blessings come down as the prayers go up,
> So build your life on the Lord.

QUESTIONS

1. Why is it important to pray?
2. How do you know it does any good to pray?
3. When can we pray? How can we pray? Where can we pray?

KIDS' COUNCIL

BRING IT HOME
- Where will you pray this week?
- What is one thing you will pray about this week?
- What is one thing you want your friends to help you pray about this week?

SHARE AND PRAY
- Ask children to share their concerns and pray for each other.
- Thank God for hearing us and answering us when we pray.
- Ask God to help us remember that we can talk to him anytime and anywhere.

ADULT STUDY QUESTIONS
- Why did Jesus have special prayer times?
- Do you have special prayer times? If so, has it been easy to be consistent with it? If not, what makes it difficult?
- Do you have any helpful hints about establishing and keeping up a special prayer time?
- What is the greatest benefit you receive from prayer?

SNACK AND FELLOWSHIP

Morning Fruit Snack. Serve a variety of fresh fruits. Provide yogurt and granola for toppings. Ask people if they ever eat or drink anything while they are having their prayer time or quiet time each day. If so, what do they like to eat or drink?

SESSION 14

Persecution

OBJECTIVE: *To learn what persecution means as well as how and why to endure it.*

■ ■ ■

WORSHIP

Sing praise and worship songs as well as songs about God's strength in times of trouble. Here are some suggestions.

"Greater Is He That Is in Me"
"I Will Call Upon the Lord"
"I'm in the Lord's Army"
"Jesus, Mighty God"
"Stand Up, Stand Up for Jesus"
"The Battle Belongs to the Lord"
"The Lord Is My Shepherd"
"You Are My Hiding Place"

STORY

The Beatitudes, Matthew 5:1-12

■ Crowds gather around Jesus to hear him teach.
■ Jesus goes up on a mountainside and sits down.
■ Jesus teaches about the type of people who will be blessed.

Make a copy of the Beatitudes. Cut them into separate strips and give one to each of nine people. Let these people take turns reading their part of the passage.

MEMORY VERSE

"Blessed are you when people insult you, persecute you and falsely say all kinds of evil against you because of me. Rejoice and be glad, because great is your reward in heaven" (Matthew 5:11, 12).

Help people remember this verse by writing phrases on separate sheets of paper and pinning one phrase to the shirt front of eight people. Choose two other people to quickly arrange the eight people in order when you say "Go." Then ask the eight people to sit down in order and say their phrases. When the verse is arranged correctly, ask each of the phrase holders to stand up one at a time, starting from the beginning of the verse. As each phrase holder stands, the rest of the group reads the phrase aloud. After his phrase is read, the phrase holder sits down. Do this over and over again with the phrase holders standing up and sitting down faster and faster each time, challenging the readers to read the verse faster and faster.

Phrases: Blessed are you/when people insult you,/persecute you/and falsely say all kinds of evil against you/because of me./Rejoice and be glad,/because great is your reward/in heaven.

56

ACTIVITIES

Choose one or more of the following activities to support the story or theme and to provide a springboard for discussion.

PAPER PLATE DOVES. Draw lines through a paper plate to divide it into eighths, as if cutting a pie. Number the sections 1–8. Now cut out sections 2, 4, 6, and 8, being careful not to cut through the very center of the plate. The remaining sections should be connected at the center. Leaving section 1 connected, cut it into an oval with one end connected to the other sections, the other end coming to a point. This is the dove's head. Sections 3 and 7 are wings, 5 is the tail. You may hang it from a string if you want. Discuss Matthew 10:16.

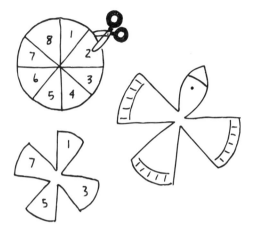

PAUL AND SILAS. Act out the story of Paul and Silas in prison, Acts 16:16-40. The narrator reads the account from the Bible while the actors pantomime the actions. When the earthquake comes, audience and actors sway back and forth as if there is an earthquake. Sound effects people may pat the floor rapidly to make a rumble while this is going on.
Option: Children act out any Bible story of persecution, speaking the parts, and adults guess which story it is. Adults then may act out a Bible story of persecution, and the children guess which story it is. You may even place the story into a modern-day setting. Choose from Peter in jail (Acts 12), Paul escapes from Damascus (Acts 9:23-25), Paul and Silas in prison (Acts 16:16-40).

EXERCISE. Jog in place. Time participants. Ask: "How long can you jog in place?" Do bent-knee sit ups. Ask: "How many can you do?" Discuss endurance, not only in the physical sense but also in the emotional and spiritual sense. Read and discuss James 1:2–4.

BE ATTITUDES BOOKMARK. Give each person a strip of heavy paper or thin cardboard about 1½ by 8 inches. Along the strip, ask each person to draw symbols representing each of the Beatitudes. For example: poor in spirit (an empty pocket), mourn (a teardrop), meek, gentle (a hand), hunger (a mouth), merciful (a rainbow), pure in heart (a heart), peacemakers (a dove), persecuted (a cross). Discuss each of the character qualities that God calls blessed.

QUESTIONS

1. Does everyone like people who believe in Jesus? What do some people think about believers?
2. What is persecution?
3. What is the person who persecutes others likely to think when people stand up for their beliefs? Discuss the witness of someone who is persecuted.
4. What is God's plan for people who suffer for him? See Matthew 5:11, 12.

KIDS' COUNCIL

BRING IT HOME

- Is there a way in which you are being persecuted now?
- Does anyone laugh at you or make fun of you for what you believe?
- Is there anything you can do or think that will help you when you are being persecuted?
- What will you do this week to help yourself or someone else endure persecution?

SHARE AND PRAY

- Ask children to share their concerns and pray for each other.
- Ask God to help us endure persecution when it comes.
- Ask God to help us forgive those who persecute us.
- Thank God for the courage to stand up for what's right.

ADULT STUDY QUESTIONS

- Read and discuss James 1:2-4. How can troubles and persecutions be occasions for joy?
- Read and discuss Hebrews 12:1-3. What does this passage tell us to do to prevent growing weary and losing heart?
- How does persecution and suffering test our purpose? our faith? our desire to please others? our way of life?

SNACK AND FELLOWSHIP

Cook both instant pudding and non-instant pudding. Ask: "Which takes patience?" Name other instant things. Name appliances that help us do things quickly. Adults might tell how it was done in years past. Ask: "Are problems able to be solved instantly?" Discuss the character quality of endurance.

SESSION 15

Letting Your Light Shine

OBJECTIVE: *To encourage each other to behave in ways that will attract people to God.*

■ ■ ■

WORSHIP

Sing praise and worship songs as well as songs about doing good that are familiar and meaningful to your group. Here are some suggestions.

"Oh, Be Careful, Little Eyes"
"Shine, Jesus, Shine"
"Stand Up, Stand Up for Jesus"
"This Is My Story"
"This Little Light of Mine"
"You Have Called Us"

STORY

Jesus' Teaching on Salt and Light, Matthew 5:13-16

■ Jesus sits on the side of a mountain.
■ Jesus teaches about how people can be like salt to the earth.
■ Jesus teaches about how people can be like light to the world.

Pour a pile of salt onto a paper plate as you read about salt. Turn off the lights and use a candle or flashlight as you read about light.

MEMORY VERSE

"Let your light shine before men, that they may see your good deeds and praise your Father in heaven" (Matthew 5:16).

Help the children remember the verse by using hand motions.

Let your light shine before men (hold up one finger as a candle)
that they may see your good deeds (form hands like binoculars around eyes)
and praise your Father in heaven (arms stretched up in praise)

ACTIVITIES

Choose one or more of the following activities to support the story or theme and to provide a springboard for discussion.

HALOS. Cut yellow construction paper, or plain white paper, into strips about ½ by 4 inches. Let everyone make these into paper chains by forming one strip into a ring. Tape or staple ends together. Loop the next strip through the ring. Tape its ends to form a second link in the chain. Continue until the chain is long enough to fit onto their heads comfortably. Tape it to make a headband. Tell how artists once drew halos above heads of people and angels to show they were godly. Ask: "How can we show people today that we love God? What can they see in our lives that might make them want to be in God's kingdom?"

MAGNETS. Place paper clips or pins on a paper plate or thin piece of cardboard. Hold the plate or cardboard out so everyone can take turns placing a magnet underneath and moving clips around on the plate. Then see how many clips or pins you can pick up with the magnet. Ask: "What else will the magnet stick to?" If you have two magnets, watch the like ends (N-N or S-S) repel and the opposite ends (N-S) attract. Talk about the word *attract*. Read Titus 2:9, 10. Ask: "Does the way we act attract people to God? What can we do to attract more people?"

LIGHT TAG HIDE AND SEEK. Choose one person to be IT. Give him a flashlight. Select a spot to be home base. Everyone hides. IT looks for the others. When he sees someone, he calls out that person's name. That person then tries to run to home base without being tagged. He's tagged if IT shines the light on him. Read the Scripture. Talk about how we are like a light and can make God's kingdom attractive to others.

FLAMES. An adult must do this or supervise closely. Light a short candle. Turn a transparent glass jar upside down and set it down over the candle. Ask: "What happens? (When the oxygen runs out, the flame goes out.) If we are like lights for God, what is our fuel? How can we keep shining?"

GOOD DEEDS. Plan a good deed that you can do as a group together. It could be yard work for an elderly or sick person, taking dinner to a shut-in person, a night of child-sitting for a single mom or dad so they can go out, and so on. Set a date and do this good deed together.

QUESTIONS

1. What are some things Christians might do that would not attract people to God but would repel them?
2. What is it about God's kingdom that is attractive to you? How can you show that to your friends?
3. Tell about someone you know who is a light for God, someone who makes God's kingdom attractive. What can we do to make God's good news attractive?

KIDS' COUNCIL

BRING IT HOME
- Is there someone in your school who watches you and sees you as an example? Is there someone in your family who sees you as an example? What can you do to influence these people for good?
- Name someone who has been a good influence (light) on you.
- How will you "let your light shine" this week?

SHARE AND PRAY
- Ask the children to share their concerns and pray for each other.
- Ask God to help them be good examples.
- Thank God for people who are good examples to them.

ADULT STUDY QUESTIONS
- Read and discuss Titus 2:9, 10. Could this apply to your influence on the job? How? What can you do to make the teaching about God attractive?
- Who has been the greatest "salt" and "light" in your life? What did he do or say to influence you?
- Read John 1:1-5 and 2 Corinthians 4:5, 6. What does this say about the source of the light that is to shine from us?

SNACK AND FELLOWSHIP

A Candle to Eat. Cut bananas in half, one half for each person. Stand each half on end on a plate (you may have to cut some of the end off to make it straighter so it will stand). Let each person put a small spoonful of yogurt or whipped cream on top of the banana, and place a maraschino cherry on top of that. The banana is the candle and the cherry is the flame.

Enjoy all the titles in Karyn Henley's new *Families Learning Together* series!

FAMILIES LEARNING TOGETHER SERIES

Karyn Henley. The new *Families Learning Together* series makes learning about the life of Christ a family affair! Each book contains 15 sessions for intergenerational groups in such settings as family nights, Sunday school, small groups, cell groups and family home study. The four titles are:

BOOK 1: JESUS' EARLY LIFE (42055)
BOOK 2: JESUS, OUR TEACHER (42056)
BOOK 3: JESUS, HEALER AND HELPER (42057)
BOOK 4: JESUS' LAST WEEK (42058)

KARYN HENLEY *is an award-winning children's communicator and author of God's Story, The Beginner's Bible and co-author of My First Hymnal. Karyn also has created a number of teaching resources, such as Child-Sensitive Teaching, Creative Bible Learning: Arts and Crafts, Creative Bible Learning: Science and Cooking and a series of file-folder curriculum units for children's ministry from Standard Publishing.*

Also new!

FUN FAMILY FESTIVALS

24 Super Celebrations for Family Ministry
Nanette Goings. Looking for creative things to do to bring church families together? *Fun Family Festivals* is great for family learning and entertainment. It's a valuable resource packed with ideas for 24 family events/celebrations that are easy to organize and sponsor. (03573)

All of these great resources are awaiting your family at your local Christian bookstore!